IPSWICH
The changing face of the town

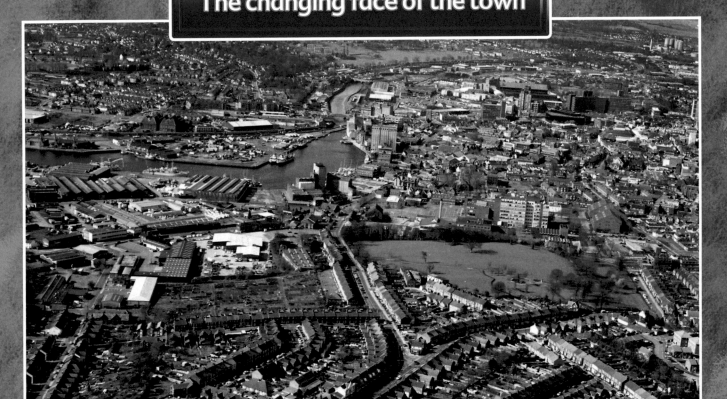

David Kindred

Old Pond
PUBLISHING LTD

Acknowledgements

My thanks to everyone who has given me access to the photographs that have been used in this book. It is often the case that albums filled with prints, boxes of negatives and colour transparencies contain images that have been unseen for decades and are in danger of falling by the wayside. Fortunately, there are people who share my interest in seeing the work of photographers brought back to life – it is to these people whom I am most grateful.

I extend my special thanks to Barbara Cutting who shared with me a set of beautiful Victorian photographs by Harry Walters, a member of her family and avid Ipswich photographer; Alan Valentine who sent me his carefully catalogued transparencies of 1960s Ipswich; and the staff of the Colchester and Ipswich Museum who gave me access to photographs of Ipswich in the 1930s taken by the museum's former curator Guy Maynard.

Stuart Grimwade of Ipswich Maritime Trust has been very helpful in providing photographs and information from the trust's archive. I am grateful to Roger Dedman for the use of his father Harry's photographs, to Carl Bartz for the Reavell's photographs, as well as to Terry Hunt, the editor of the *East Anglian Daily Times*, and Nigel Pickover, the editor of the *Evening Star*, for pictures from the newspapers' archives. Thanks also to Jack Keen, Frank Symonds, Bob Graham, Fred Bridges, Jenny Catchpole, Nick Wiggin, Stephen Cordrey and Mike Farthing.

A special mention must be made to the memory of the late Doug Cotton for the Titshall Brothers' photographs and to Charlie Girling, whose work I have included. I have done my best to credit the work of photographers when their identities are known.

A busy workshop at Ransomes, Sims and Jefferies engineering works in 1916. Charles Packard (centre foreground) was typical of many who spent their entire working lives with the company. He worked for the company from the age of fourteen for fifty-one years. Often several generations of the same family worked there. 'RS&J' occupied a large site around Duke Street (see page 109) until moving to Nacton Road during the 1960s.

Contents

Ipswich Today

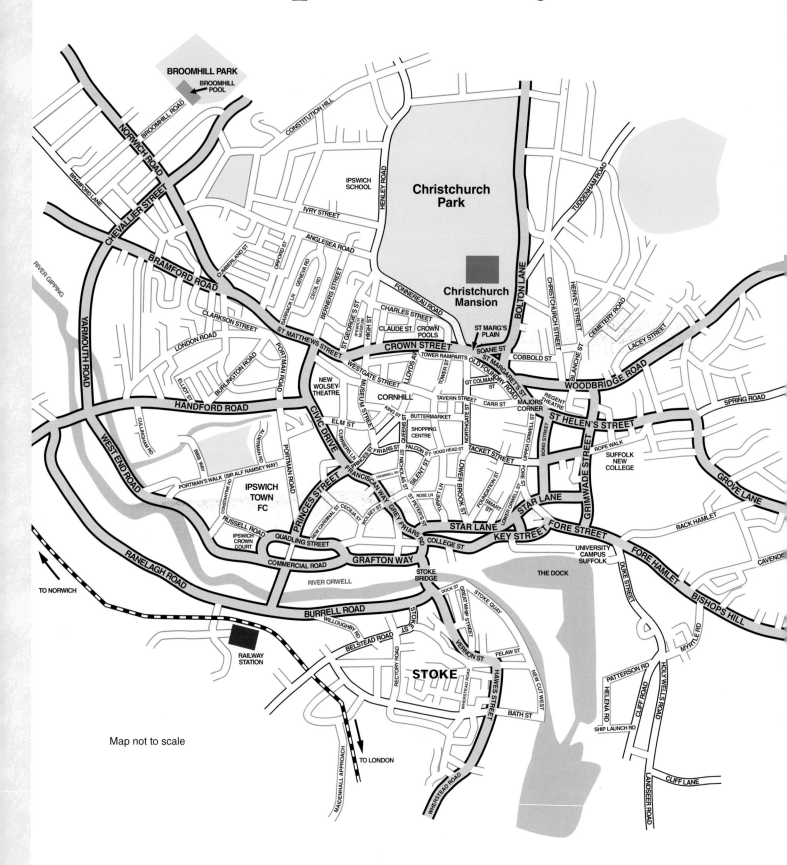

Map not to scale

The start of a costers' race at the junction of Colman Street (background) and Old Foundry Road. The race, which ran along Woodbridge Road, was a popular bank holiday event prior to World War I. The building in the left foreground belonged to Rands and Jeckell tent makers. These buildings were demolished in the redevelopment of the area in the mid-1960s. The spire of St Mary-le-Tower Church is top right.

Preface

Location photography, including a record of the streets of our town, became practical in the 1880s when companies like Kodak produced dry plates, made mostly of glass. They replaced the cumbersome 'wet plates' that had to be coated, exposed at once and then developed while still wet.

So the earliest photographs in this book are from the 1880s. Other early images include high-quality ones taken by Harry Walters, a photographer who worked in Ipswich from the 1890s until 1926. Most of his photographs were taken to record events such as the celebrations of Queen Victoria's Diamond Jubilee in 1897. These images show the streets and buildings of Ipswich town as they were at that time.

Guy Maynard, curator of the Ipswich Museum in the 1930s, was interested in recording the areas in Ipswich where changes were planned. Maynard specifically focused on the poor housing areas of the town – areas such as Cox Lane, 'The Potteries' and 'The Mount'. Not only did Maynard record the buildings before their demolition, but also the people in the streets, bringing the scenes to life.

Amateur photographers attending events or taking pictures of their own specialist subjects are often unwittingly responsible for helping to record changes to a particular area. One such photographer, Alan Valentine, took a keen interest in photographing transport and as a bonus recorded the changing town in the background. Valentine also meticulously recorded the dates on which the photos were

taken – a detail that is often overlooked but incredibly valuable when attempting to chronicle a changing past.

Going area by area, I have grouped photographs from different periods to show how the town has been continually evolving. For example, on one set of pages I have focused on the part now known as Giles Circus, illustrating how much that area, named in memory of the famous cartoonist, has changed since the Victorian period including photographs from 1903 when the streets were widened to accommodate the electric tram service.

Many of the pictures in this book chronicle the architectural choices of the 1960s. St Matthews Street and Carr Street, in particular, are areas of Ipswich where grey, concrete 1960s buildings virtually wiped out the ornate structures that had stood there before them.

The Ipswich dock area is another part of town that has been well recorded by professional and amateur photographers alike. Completely transformed from commercial dock to residential and leisure area, the modern waterfront now boasts a university building on the site of a former grain silo complex.

Technological advances in photography have greatly improved our ability to make comparisons with the past through pictures. My only hope is that some of the hundreds of thousands of images that are now captured daily with digital cameras will survive as long as the images previously taken on film.

David Kindred, 2011

The Town Centre

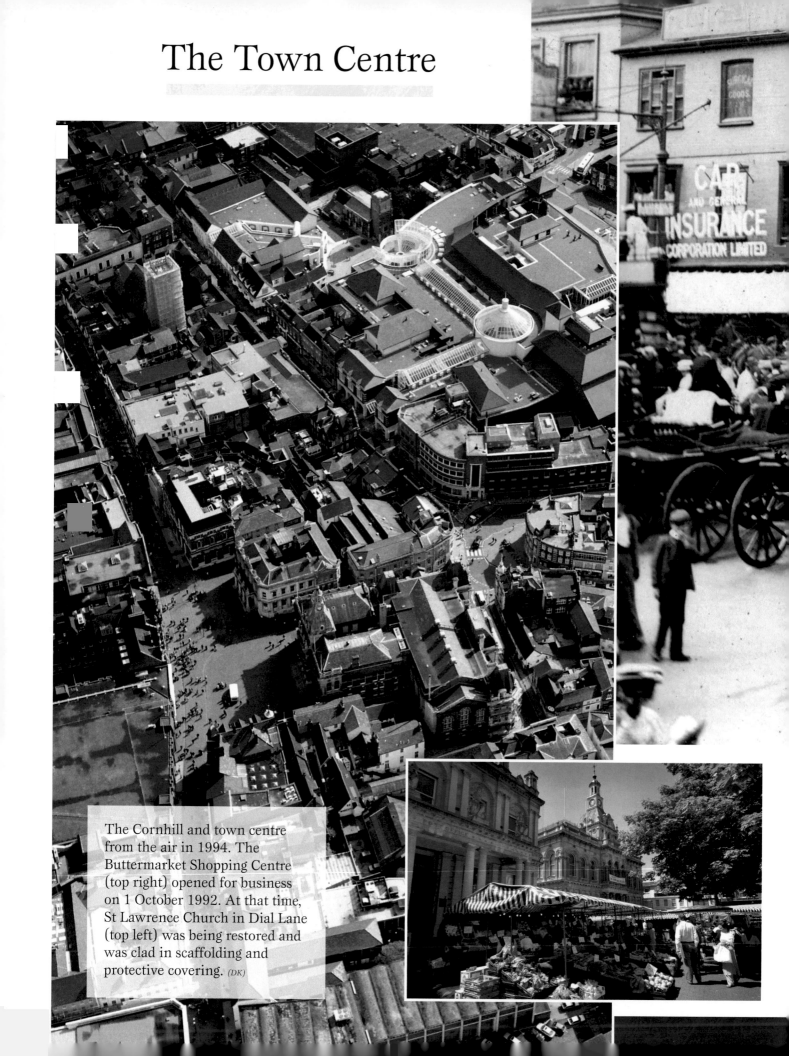

The Cornhill and town centre from the air in 1994. The Buttermarket Shopping Centre (top right) opened for business on 1 October 1992. At that time, St Lawrence Church in Dial Lane (top left) was being restored and was clad in scaffolding and protective covering. *(DK)*

◄

The Cornhill and the market in 2006. The building on the left was built to be a post office. It opened in 1881 on the site of the Corn Exchange building which had been erected in 1849. The Town Hall, built by local builder Edward Gibbons for just under £12,000, opened in January 1868. *(DK)*

The Cornhill in 1907 with an electric tram in the centre. The South African War Memorial, unveiled at this location the year before, was pulled on rollers to Christchurch Park in 1924 by about fifty men. Limmer's grocery store is to the left of the tram.

The Cornhill circa 1894. The horse-drawn trams ran from 1880 until the
electric trams came into service in 1903. The cabman's shelter in the centre
was built in 1893. In 1895, it was removed to Christchurch Park where it was
placed near the Bolton Lane gate. After being damaged by fire in 1995 it was
restored and placed close to the Westerfield Road gate in 2006.

The imposing building behind the shelter was built in 1889 and primarily used
by the bank of Bacon, Cobbold and Tollemache. It was designed by local
architect T W Cotman. Other businesses operating from the building were the
watchmakers W H Collis and Son and ironmongers Pells and Suggate. The
building on the left was the National and Provincial Bank of England. *(William Vick)*

The Cornhill in the mid-1890s from Westgate Street. Grimwade's store (right) had gas lamps hanging from the building to light window displays. The building in the left background was replaced in 1933. (Author)

Debenhams Store (former Footmans site)

Work began on cutting the Lloyds Avenue arch through to the Cornhill in 1929. The arch opened to traffic on 5 January 1930. This photograph was taken in 2005. (DK)

The Cornhill looking towards Westgate Street in 1909. The outfitter business of J and H Grimwade was opened in Westgate Street by Richard Grimwade in 1844. In 1879, John Henry Grimwade acquired the former Bell Inn site on the corner of the Cornhill and built a new shop. The premises were extended along the Cornhill in 1904. Grimwade's closed in 1996.

Crowds lined the streets of Ipswich in April 1968 to watch airmen march in celebration of the 50th anniversary of the formation of the RAF. This photograph was taken as the ranks of airmen from RAF Wattisham marched across the Cornhill. Twenty Lightning aircraft roared over the town as the deputy mayor, Mrs Marjorie Keeble, took the salute. This photograph was taken from Grimwade's shop.

In June 1930, the Cornhill was packed with crowds of people when the Prince of Wales – who abdicated in December 1936 as the uncrowned Edward VIII – visited Ipswich to officially open the town's new airport. This photograph was taken as he arrived at the Town Hall.

The businesses with the sun blinds, in the background, included Burton's tailors; Dunn and Company hatters; Freeman, Hardy and Willis boot and shoe shop; H Samuel jewellers and the Picture House and Café. A pair of single-deck trolley buses built by Ransomes, Sims and Jefferies were stuck in the crowd.

Tavern Street from the Cornhill in the early 1930s.
The bank building on the right was built in 1928.
The trolley bus was built in Ipswich by Ransomes,
Sims and Jefferies in 1930. The two policemen at
the junction with Lloyds Avenue were about to
swap traffic control duty. *(Frederick Gillson)*

Tavern Street in December 1965 with Joe Lyons' restaurant on the right and Frederick Corder's store on the left. *(Terry Neeves)*

A view of mid-1930s Tavern Street from near the junction with Dial Lane (left) and Tower Street (right). The buildings on the right were due to be demolished when this photograph was taken. (See picture on page 14.) The spire on the Picture House cinema, which opened on 14 December 1910 and closed in 1958, is at the end of the buildings on the right. *(Guy Maynard, Colchester and Ipswich Museum Service)*

Tavern Street, from near St Lawrence Lane looking towards the Cornhill in 1897. Hatton Court is to the right. *(Harry Walters)*

Tavern Street in 1897. The buildings on the left at the corner of Tower Street were ticket offices for the Great Eastern Railway Company. The shop in the centre was Frederick Fish and Son's Suffolk House store, merchant drapers and house furnishers. *(Harry Walters)*

A view of the impressive window displays of J and J Edwards' outfitters shop in Tavern Street around 1904. This shop closed in 1968.

A similar view of Tavern Street in October 2010. *(DK)*

Road works at White Horse Corner circa 1900. The photographer
was in Carr Street. Tavern Street is in the background. The Great
White Horse Hotel, on the right, lost its timbered front in 1818 when
the road was widened. J and J Edwards' store (on page 16) was in the
building beyond the Great White Horse.

Upper Brook Street from White Horse Corner around 1904. The buildings between Tavern Street and the Buttermarket were demolished when the road was widened a few years later. The buildings on the right, which were occupied for many years by Croydon's jewellers shop, were re-fronted in 1931. *(Harry Walters)*

Upper Brook Street in January 1965. This view is similar to the photograph above showing how the buildings on the right of the street were altered to widen the road.

The buildings in Upper Brook Street, between the Buttermarket (left) and Tavern Street, were demolished when the road was widened early in the 20th century. The main building featured on the corner of the Buttermarket was Symonds' chemists shop. *(Harry Walters)*

A similar view of Upper Brook Street taken on 21 January 2011. *(DK)*

A Victorian photograph of the Buttermarket from near the junction with Upper Brook Street. Some of the buildings on the left were destroyed by fire in August 1992 (see page 21). The Ancient House is at the far end of the buildings on the left.

A similar view of the Buttermarket in October 2010. *(DK)*

A Victorian photograph of the Ancient House in the Buttermarket. William Sparrowe took over the house in 1591 and members of his family owned it for almost 300 years. Robert Sparrowe decorated the front of his home with pargeting possibly to commemorate the restoration of the monarchy soon before a visit by Charles II in 1668. The building on the left was the Wagon and Horses public house, which dated from the 16th century. It closed in 1935 and a cinema was built on the site. (See page 22.)

A fire destroyed buildings in the Buttermarket on 2 August 1992. The blaze hit Hughes TV shop and Alderton's shoe shop. A neighbouring book shop was badly damaged and had to be demolished. *(DK, EADT/Evening Star)*

The close proximity of the Buttermarket fire to the Ancient House is illustrated in this photograph. *(DK, EADT/Evening Star)*

The ABC cinema is in the centre of this view of the Buttermarket, taken in 1985. The site became part of the Buttermarket Shopping Centre (see page 21). The cinema closed in April 1986. *(Jack Keen)*

The buildings in the centre of this 1930s photograph of the Buttermarket were set back and refaced. Work on the timbered building was carried out by Frederick Tibbenham Ltd of Ipswich. The alterations were finished around 1934. *(W 'Billy' Robinson)*

The Buttermarket in the mid-1960s from near Dial Lane. In order from left to right, the shops used to be: R Barratt jewellers, A Croasdale chemist, Murdoch's domestic appliances and record shop, James Parnell's shoe shop, A Rawling optician, Limmer and Pipe restaurant and Cowell's department store.

The Buttermarket in the late 1980s. W S Cowell's store was built in 1892 and was demolished soon after this photograph was taken. The site was cleared for the building of the Buttermarket Shopping Centre. Market Lane (right), which led to Falcon Street, was lost to redevelopment. *(Charlie Girling)*

The Buttermarket from the junction of Queen Street (right) and Princes Street in June 1930. The photograph was taken when the town was decorated for a visit by the Prince of Wales (see page 11). The entrance to the Buttermarket was widened in the mid-1930s when the building line on the left was set back (see page 22). The main building on the right held the offices of the Alliance Assurance Company. On the extreme right is part of the Queens Hotel. The buildings on the left included the premises of Hinsley H Burgham optician, Clifford Collins chemist and Bantoft and Higgs ladies and gentlemen's tailors. *(Titshall Brothers)*

The same view as above in March 2011. *(DK)*

Falcon Street in 1934. The man in the centre is walking past Market Lane, which connected to the Buttermarket. The building on the left, beyond the gates, was demolished in May 1935 and became part of Cowell's printing works as their site off Market Lane expanded. The Buttermarket Shopping Centre was built on this site.

A similar view of Falcon Street in April 2011. *(DK)*

This aerial photograph was taken in May 1989, just before construction started on the Buttermarket Shopping Centre. St Mary-le-Tower Church is located on the top right. The Town Hall and Corn Exchange are centre left.

➤

The Buttermarket Shopping Centre from the air in March 1994. The centre opened for trade in October 1992. At the time of the opening major shops at the complex included C&A and Owen Owen. St Mary-le-Tower Church is top left. (DK)

The Sickle Inn was on the site where the Corn Exchange was built (see page 29).

The junction of Princes Street and the Buttermarket has completely changed since this photograph was taken in 1901. The junction was widened to accommodate the tracks of the new electric tram service. Lines of the horse-drawn service were still in Princes Street but there were plans to turn another line into Queen Street with a sweeping 'S' bend. In order to do this, more space was needed so these buildings were demolished and the new ones set further back. The establishment to the right of Beard's bedding store was Albert Bond's wine and spirits store. King Street is the road on the right. *(Harry Walters)*

The Corn Exchange from the junction of Queen Street and the Buttermarket soon after it opened. The cornerstone of the building was laid on 22 October 1880 and the opening ceremony was held on 26 July 1882. For ninety years the building served as a corn and provisions market as well as a venue for events. The building was altered between 1972 and 1975 when it opened as an entertainment centre.

Giles Circus in March 2011. The statue of the characters from cartoons by Carl Giles was unveiled in 1993 by actor Warren Mitchell. It was moved to a new plinth in 2010 when the area was refurbished. The character 'Grandma' faces where Giles' studio was at the end of the Buttermarket, the site where he produced his cartoons for the *Daily Express* and *Sunday Express*. *(DK)*

Carr Street in April 1966: featuring the offices and printing works of the *East Anglian Daily Times* on the corner of Little Colman Street. The company had operated here since 1887. This photograph was taken a few weeks before the company, publishers of the *Evening Star* and several weekly newspapers, moved to a new building in Lower Brook Street. This red brick building was demolished and replaced with a shopping centre. *(Alan Valentine)*

The same part of Carr Street on October 2010. *(DK)*

Carr Street in the late 1880s with the Cross Keys Hotel on the left. This 16th century building was converted into an inn in the 17th century and was an important establishment in coaching days with large stables at the rear. When the street was widened in 1890, a new Cross Keys was built on the site. The building has been a shop for many years and there is still a footpath – once know as Cross Keys Lane – alongside the building. The lines in the street were for the horse-drawn tram service, which started in the town in 1880 and ran through Carr Street from 1884.

Carr Street in February 1964 from near White Horse Corner. The street was then open to traffic and was part of a bus route. Included in the shops on the right are Heppel's chemist, Lavey's outfitters, Hawkins and Son cotton goods shop and MacFisheries. On the left were Hubbards jewellers and the East Anglian Daily Times Company premises.

Carr Street in the mid-1930s as a shop was being refitted for Curry's electrical store. Other shops included Dewhurst's butchers and F W Woolworth. The first building beyond Woolworth's was the Cross Keys Hotel which closed in the late 1930s (see page 31).

Carr Street looking towards Majors Corner in 1990. *(DK)*

Carr Street from Majors Corner circa 1930. The Beehive public house, owned by the Tollemache brewery, is on the corner. This establishment opened in 1899 though the

Tudor style of the building gave the impression that it was much older. The Beehive was demolished in 1960. *(Frederick Gillson)*

The same view as above in 1990. The building which replaced the Beehive public house has been a supermarket, shop and restaurant. *(DK)*

This red brick building at the junction of Carr Street and Old Foundry Road, photographed in around 1904, was home to a Singer sewing machine shop, Stollery's family grocers and the Provincial Dyeing and Cleaning Company. The public house on the left of the shops is the Salutation, which opened in the 17th century. *(Harry Walters)*

James Redstone's store (left), which sold 'fancy goods and toys', was at the corner of Carr Street and Cox Lane. This timber-framed building was dismantled in 1907, exhibited in London and then rebuilt in Northamptonshire where it was destroyed by fire. The building was sold at auction on the understanding it would be removed in 21 days. The first bid was for just £5, the second for £30 and it finally sold to a builder named Mr Harris for £75. The Ipswich Co-operative Society drapery department opened on the site in February 1908. The Co-op store and offices were built in 1886. This photograph was taken around 1890. *(William Vick)*

Majors Corner from Upper Orwell Street in the early 20th century. St Helen's Street is off to the right and St Margaret's Street and Carr Street are to the left. The Beehive public house is on the extreme left. All the buildings featured in this photo are no longer there. *(Harry Walters)*

This battery tower wagon, built by Ransomes, Sims and Jefferies, was being used to take down the trolley bus cables at Majors Corner in September 1963. The same vehicle, with solid tyres, was used to install the cables for the trolley buses in the 1920s. The shops in the white-fronted building included W Broughhall's shoe repair company, Sarony's photographers and Avis Cook Ltd television and radio engineers. These buildings were demolished in 1968.
(Alan Valentine)

St Margaret's Street from near Majors Corner in November 1933. In the background is the junction with Colman Street and Woodbridge Road. *(Guy Maynard, Colchester and Ipswich Museum Service)*

Some of the buildings in St Margaret's Street between Majors Corner and Woodbridge Road survived into the 1960s. When this photograph was taken in the 1930s this was a busy group of small shops including H Sugar greengrocer, Herbert Havell gramophone dealers and Leonard Payne's ladies and gentleman's hairdressers. Botwood's garage is on the extreme right (see page 37).

(Guy Maynard, Colchester and Ipswich Museum Service)

Majors Corner in the early 1960s.
Botwood's garage (right) was
demolished and an Odeon cinema
was opened on the site in March
1991. When this photograph was
taken, the centre of the junction
had a huge steel post in the
middle supporting trolley bus
wires and traffic lights. *(Harry Dedman)*

A trolley bus approaches a stop
in St Margaret's Street in
February 1963. On the left is
Botwood's garage. St Helens
Street is in the background.
(Alan Valentine)

St Margaret's Green and church in 1895. The horse and wagon on the right are entering from Cobbold Street. The building at the far end of those on the left was the Saracens Head public house, which had been there since the 17th century. It closed in November 1960.
(Harry Walters)

The buildings at the junction of St Margaret's Green and St Margaret's Street were demolished soon after this photograph was taken in 1935. The shop on the corner had been the premises of Charles Crisp boot maker. The garage on the right was extended to occupy the whole site. It was demolished between April and May 2011. The building on the left was then Philips and Piper's clothing factory. In May 1984, the building was reopened as flats and renamed Pipers Court.
(Guy Maynard, Colchester and Ipswich Museum Service)

A busy day on St Margaret's Plain from Northgate Street in 1897. The Running Buck public house at the junction of Soane Street was flying flags as the town celebrated the Diamond Jubilee of Queen Victoria. The Running Buck was one of Ipswich's most ancient inns; it was listed as one of twenty-four in the town in 1689. *(Harry Walters)*

The junction of Soane Street (left) and St Margaret's Street from St Margaret's Plain in 1933. The buildings in the centre had recently been altered to widen the entrance of St Margaret's Street. The two right-hand gables were demolished and three gables built to face St Margaret's Street. The architect, John Sherman of Northgate Street, also designed the frontage of the building opposite the Great White Horse Hotel in Tavern Street, which was the premises of Croydon's the jewellers at the time. The building work was carried out by Sadler and Son Ltd. *(Guy Maynard, Colchester and Ipswich Museum Service)*

The world famous Barnam and Bailey circus visited Ipswich in 1898 and
1899. This photograph was taken in 1899 from the yard of the Halberd
public house as a huge team of horses pulled a wagon and band in Fonnereau
Road. The buildings on the right are shown in the photograph on page 41.
(Harry Walters)

The junction of Fonnereau Road and St Margaret's Green around 1890. After these buildings were demolished, the Bethesda Church was built. The church opened on 2 July 1913.

The Bethesda Baptist Church in March 2011. *(DK)*

Tower Ramparts in the 1880s. Houses stood on the town bank and the road inside the rampart was known as Tower Ditches until alterations in the 1930s. The area was cleared in 1934 and became a car park then a bus station. The large building in the background was

William Pretty and Sons clothing factory, which was built in 1881–2, see page 48. The Footman & Company bridge is also featured on pages 48–9. The Tower Ramparts Shopping Centre was built on the left of this view.

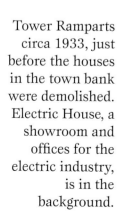

Tower Ramparts circa 1933, just before the houses in the town bank were demolished. Electric House, a showroom and offices for the electric industry, is in the background.

Crown Street in 1934 looking towards Northgate Street. This photograph was taken from the corner of William Street near the Cricketers Hotel.
(W 'Billy' Robinson)

The junction of William Street and Crown Street in the mid-1930s. When this photograph was taken, the Cricketers Hotel had recently been built and the Millers Arms on the left was due to be demolished. In May 1984, Crown Pools opened near this site.

Tower Ramparts from St Mary-le-Tower Church around 1908. The building in the foreground opened in September 1899 as the High Elementary Secondary School for boys. Later it became the Municipal Secondary School for boys and much later the Tower Ramparts Secondary Modern School. William Pretty's clothing factory is centre left (see page 48). The houses on Fitzroy Street, Beck Street, Chenery Street, Charles Street and William Street are in the centre. Most of those houses were demolished in 1966. Crown Pools was built in the centre of this view but when this photograph was taken the site belonged to a maltings owned by R Paul.

Beck Street in 1939. Most of the houses in this area – including Charles Street, Fitzroy Street, Chenery Street and Peel Street – were demolished in the summer of 1966. Crown Pools, some offices and a car park were built on most of this site.

(Guy Maynard, Colchester and Ipswich Museum Service)

MY OLD SCHOOL ON THESE PAGES

During the 1970s the site formerly occupied by Egerton's garage was used by the market. On 24 April 1982, the foundation stone was laid for Crown Pools and the complex was formally opened in May 1984. Tower Ramparts School, in the background, opened in 1906. It was demolished in 1979. In its place the Tower Ramparts Shopping Centre was erected and opened to customers on 7 November 1986.

Demolition work at Tower Ramparts School in 1979.

Crown Street in the early 1930s. Crown Pools was built to the right of this view. Electric House is in the background to the left.
(Guy Maynard, Colchester and Ipswich Museum Service)

A pair of Ipswich buses at Tower Ramparts in 1962. Trolley buses, like the one on the left, were taken out of service in August 1963. The Odeon Cinema at the top of Lloyds Avenue opened in 1936. *(Harry Dedman)*

Crown Street in September 1962. In the background is Egerton's garage which was built in 1928 with 100,000 feet of floor space and enlarged in 1940. One of the town's trolley buses was passing the Cricketers Hotel. *(Alan Valentine)*

A similar view of Crown Street in February 2011. *(DK)*

The site of William Pretty's works at Tower Ramparts in 1930. The company was founded as a cottage industry in 1820. It made corsets in Ipswich using mainly outworkers and was the oldest corset manufacturing business in the country.

In the early days it was run by Footman, Pretty and Nicholson. The company expanded and had this four-storey works built at Tower Ramparts in 1881. With a staff of about 1,500 they had a monopoly on corset and lingerie production until the 1940s but the company was eventually taken over in 1968 by Courtaulds who reduced the staff to 350. By 1982, just before closure, there were only eighty-two people left working at the site.

The building was partly demolished in 1983 and finally disappeared in 1987 when it became a car park. William Pretty's works is remembered for providing its employees with benefits that were unrivalled at that time. The company managed to remain one of the main employers of women in the area until Courtaulds ran the business down. It has been said that thousands of girls used to leave school on a Friday and start work in the factory the following Monday. Many of them came from Tower Ramparts Secondary Modern School just a few hundred yards away.

Staff at William Pretty's works at Tower Ramparts in January 1972.

A footbridge connected the William Pretty factory and Footman Pretty's 'Waterloo House' store, which was between Tower Ramparts and Westgate Street. The store was rebuilt in the early 1980s and became Debenhams.

The entrance to Footman's store in Lloyds Avenue in the 1930s.

High Street from the junction with Crown Street in 1933. The Crown and Sceptre public house on the right closed in 1959 and was demolished in July 1961. All the buildings featured have gone. *(Guy Maynard, Colchester and Ipswich Museum Service)*

A similar view of High Street in February 2011. *(DK)*

The junction of St Matthews Street, Crown Street (background) and Westgate Street was packed with hundreds of people who came to see television and radio personality Simon Dee open a new Tesco Store on St Matthews Street in March 1969. All the buildings in the left background were demolished when the road was widened. The building from St George's Street to High Street had been home to Aldridge's sports outfitters, Newstead's bakery, S Blumfield confectioner, Vera Dunningham ladies hairdresser, Aquatic and Aquarium Displays, Terry Rumsey hairdresser and the Crown Street Congregational Church. *(DK, EADT/Evening Star)*

A similar view taken in February 2011.

Westgate Street looking towards the Cornhill in 1897. The Crown and Anchor and Footman's 'Waterloo House' store are on the left. The signs on the shops on the right say 'Hot and Cold Baths – Always Ready' and 'Hair Cutting – Shaving and Shampooing Saloons'. *(Harry Walters)*

Westgate Street in 1897 during the celebrations for Queen Victoria's Diamond Jubilee. This photograph was taken from close to the junction with Museum Street looking towards the Cornhill. *(Charles Emeny)*

Westgate Street looking towards St Matthews Street in the mid-1950s. Part of the ground floor of the Crown and Anchor Hotel had by then been taken over by Footman's 'Waterloo House' store, J Stones radio dealers and the Fifty Shilling Tailors.

Westgate Street in March 2011.

Westgate Street from near the junction with Crown Street and
St Matthews Street during the Diamond Jubilee celebrations for
Queen Victoria. Black Horse Lane is to the right. *(Harry Walters)*

54

Westgate Street circa 1930 from the junction with Museum Street (left) and High Street. The public house on the corner of High Street was the Barley Mow. The street was open to two-way traffic.

(Frederick Gillson)

The opposite view (from the picture above) of Westgate Street taken in the late 1890s. The tower of St Lawrence church is in the background.

(Harry Walters)

The centre of town from the air in March 1965. Civic Drive was in the
process of being built from St Matthews Street (left) towards
Princes Street (right). Excavation work for the underground spiral car park
is in the centre foreground. *(Tony Ray, EADT/Evening Star)*

The same view as the photo on page 56 taken twenty-nine years later. The New Wolsey Theatre, Civic Centre, Crown and Magistrate's courts and police station are all in the foreground of this view. In 1994, the market was on a site next to the Civic Centre. *(DK)*

St Matthews Street in 1897. The flags were flying to celebrate the Diamond Jubilee of Queen Victoria. The Queens Head public house on the right was demolished in the mid-1960s when the area was redeveloped and Civic Drive cut through to Princes Street. The photograph was taken from where the Civic Drive/Berners Street roundabout was built. All the buildings on the left were demolished when St Matthews Street was widened in the 1960s. *(Harry Walters)*

A similar view of St Matthews Street in May 1964 when the buildings on the left were being demolished. *(Alan Valentine)*

St Matthews Street looking towards the junction with Berners Street (to the right, halfway along the street). A roundabout and Civic Drive (off to the left) were built during alterations to the street in the mid-1960s. *(Harry Walters)*

The same view of St Matthews Street in September 1963 as an Eastern Counties bus heads towards Crown Street. The buildings on the right were demolished in 1964. They included Howes and Sons garage. BBC Radio Suffolk's studios were constructed near the buildings in the distant background and the station came on the air in April 1990. *(Alan Valentine)*

St Matthews Street from Westgate Street circa 1960. The Rainbow public house was at the corner of St George's Street. It closed in November 1961. *(Harry Dedman)*

A panoramic view of the St Matthews Street demolition work in April 1964. The photograph was taken from the site of the Rainbow public house at the junction of St George's Street. The buildings on the other side of the street were the premises of W J Smith's Albion House drapers and Whitelaw's general store. These buildings were replaced and a Tesco's opened on the site in March 1969 (see page 51).

A similar view in February 2011. *(DK)*

St Matthews Street in November 1962 looking towards the town centre. The first two buildings on the left survived the alterations in the 1960s. The Golden Fleece Hotel and those beyond were all demolished when the road was widened in the mid-1960s. The Golden Fleece Hotel opened in the 18th century and closed on 29 September 1962. BBC Radio Suffolk's studios were built behind where the hotel was located.

These shops at the corner of St Matthews Church Lane (left) and St Matthews Street were being demolished when this photograph was taken in the mid-1960s from where the Civic Drive/St Matthews Street roundabout was built. The shops included Leisure Hours wool shop, Stanley Fulcher furnishing fabrics, Albert Atkinson butcher and S Brewer grocer. The corner of the Queens Head public house on the left is featured in the Victorian photograph on page 58. *(Jack Keen)*

St Matthews Baths Hall in the mid-1960s after a line of shops, which stood in front, were demolished. The Baths Hall, was built between World War I and World War II, and boasted a pool measuring 75 x 30 feet. There was a balcony for 200 spectators. The building had a temporary floor over the pool in the winter so that the site could be used for meetings, exhibitions and dancing. This photograph was taken from the location of the Civic Drive roundabout looking towards Norwich Road. *(Jack Keen)*

Swimmers at St Matthews Baths in September 1965.

A Women's Institute meeting at St Matthews Baths Hall in March 1966.

The Move on stage at St Matthews Baths Hall in March 1968. This was one of the regular gigs arranged for 'Bluesville' by Ron and Nanda Lesley who promoted live music in Ipswich from 1958 for around fifteen years. *(DK, EADT/Evening Star)*

Children gathered for the camera at the junction of Little Gipping Street and Mount Street in 1933. The housing in that part of Ipswich was poor and was mostly demolished in the 1950s. The Civic Drive/Handford Road roundabout was built close to here in the mid-1960s.
(Guy Maynard, Colchester and Ipswich Museum Service)

Streets of small houses close to the Ipswich town centre were demolished in the late 1950s. The area known as 'The Mount' was located where the police station, the Wolsey Theatre and the Civic Centre were built in the 1960s and 70s. This lady was walking her dog in St Matthews Church Lane where Civic Drive is now. The chimney in the background was St Matthews Baths Hall.

The Civic Centre building in July 2007. The former Ipswich Borough Council offices were demolished in 2008. The New Wolsey Theatre is on the left of this view. (DK)

An underground spiral car park was built close to the junction with Civic Drive and Handford Road. This picture was taken in March 1966 as construction neared completion.

The spiral car park from the roof of the Civic Centre on Civic Drive in July 2007. The New Wolsey Theatre (right) opened September 1979 replacing the Arts Theatre in Tower Street, which saw its last show 'Happy End' in April 1979. The foundation stone for the New Wolsey was laid in February 1978 by Trevor Nunn, a former pupil of Northgate School and, at that time, one of the directors of the Royal Shakespeare Company. (DK)

Elm Street in April 1912. The premises of R D and J B Fraser's furniture store, cabinet works and pawnbrokers were severely damaged by fire. They stood on a site bound by Princes Street, Museum Street and Elm Street. The building was demolished and a building of similar style built on the site. The company was founded around 1833. It was taken over and traded as Fraser (Maple) Ltd until 1984. The building was converted to offices. *(Charles Trudgill)*

Queen Street from the junction with Falcon Street in the early 1930s. This photograph was taken just before the demolition of the first five buildings on the left. The new shops were set further back.
(Guy Maynard, Colchester and Ipswich Museum Service)

Queen Street in June 2011. *(DK)*

Princes Street runs from the bottom left corner of this 1950s aerial view. Portman Road, the Cattle Market (see page 146) and the football ground are in the left corner. The houses in the streets off Princes Street were demolished in the mid-1960s when the Greyfriars scheme was built. The streets include Redan Street, Metz Street, Chalon Street, Cecilia Street, Portman Street, James Street and Edgar Street. 'The Mount' (see page 64) is in the centre and Christchurch Park is top right.

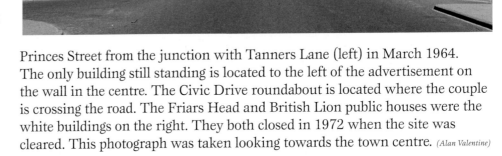

Princes Street from the junction with Tanners Lane (left) in March 1964. The only building still standing is located to the left of the advertisement on the wall in the centre. The Civic Drive roundabout is located where the couple is crossing the road. The Friars Head and British Lion public houses were the white buildings on the right. They both closed in 1972 when the site was cleared. This photograph was taken looking towards the town centre. *(Alan Valentine)*

The town centre from the air in March 1994 from over the grounds of the Ipswich Town Football Club. The Princes Street roundabout is in the bottom right corner and the Buttermarket Shopping Centre is in the centre. *(DK)*

The Willis Ltd building in July 2011. Princes Street is on the left and Franciscan Way on the right. *(DK)*

Princes Street in the late 1960s. In May 1972, work began on the glass-clad Willis building designed by Norman Foster. The £6.5 million building was opened in February 1975. Alfred Clark's leather goods dealers were on the corner of Thursby's Lane. Other buildings demolished in the redevelopment of the area included the British Lion and Friars Head public houses (see picture page 68). The Greyfriars development is in the background. *(Derek Eggleton)*

St Nicholas Street from St Peters Street in the 1890s. Cutler Street is off to the left and Silent Street to the right. The Wolsey Pharmacy at the corner of Silent Street is on the right. This Grade II listed medieval timber-framed structure is often mistakenly referred to as the birthplace of Cardinal Thomas Wolsey, who was Chancellor to King Henry VIII for fourteen years. Wolsey was born some time between 1470 and early 1471 when his parents were living in the parish of St Mary at the Elms. In October 1472, his parents moved into premises on St Nicholas Street (opposite Curson House) that housed various inns and a butcher's shop. *(Harry Walters)*

The Wolsey Pharmacy was in Curson House at the corner of Silent Street (right) and St Nicholas Street. This photograph was taken around 1895. *(Harry Walters)*

St Nicholas Street from the junction with Silent Street (right) and Cutler Street in October 1964. Curson House on the right was restored; the project was completed in 2007. A statue of Cardinal Wolsey was unveiled at the site in June 2011. *(Alan Valentine)*

Cromwell Street in October 1964. The street ran from St Nicolas Street (in the background) to Friars Road. The glass-clad Willis building was built to the left of this view. Some of the distant houses on the left are still standing. In the 1960s this area became part of Franciscan Way, taking traffic to St Nicholas Street. It was then converted into Cromwell Square car park.

(Alan Valentine)

St Nicholas Street in 2006 looking towards the town centre.

St Nicholas Street in an undated Victorian photograph probably taken in the 1880s. Cromwell Square is now located to the left where the trees were. The buildings on the right feature in the photograph taken in 2006. The building on the left is featured in the Victorian photograph on page 72.

St Nicholas Street in the 1890s.
The buildings on the right were
demolished and the Hippodrome
Theatre opened on the site in 1905.
(Harry Walters)

Dancers at the Savoy
Ballroom in 1964.

The Hippodrome Theatre, St Nicholas
Street, in April 1955. The theatre
opened in 1905 as a music hall and in
1930 it started showing films. The
building closed as a theatre in 1957. It
was converted into the Savoy Ballroom
and then into a bingo hall before being
demolished in 1985. An office block was
built on the site.

St Nicholas Street in May 1965 with the Savoy ballroom and the bingo hall in the background. *(Alan Valentine)*

St Nicholas Street from a similar viewpoint in April 2011. *(DK)*

Upper Orwell Street in the early years of the 20th century from near the junction with Eagle Street. The street and its shops were then at the centre of hundreds of houses, which stood in the Cox Lane and Rope Walk area of town. St Michael's Church, built in the early 1880s, is in the background to the right. The church was badly damaged in a fire on 7 March 2011.

The Majors Corner end of Upper Orwell Street in 1900 when the buildings on the left were due to be replaced. The new Beehive public house at the junction with Carr Street (see page 33) is at the far end of the buildings on the left. Craig Court (right) became the site of a bus stop. *(Harry Walters)*

Upper Orwell Street in 1934 from the junction with Eagle Street. *(Guy Maynard, Colchester and Ipswich Museum Service)*

The Eclipse Inn stood on the corner of Orwell Place and Upper Orwell Street selling the 'Celebrated Ales, Stout and Porter of Catchpole and Company'. When this Victorian period photograph was taken, there was a public house on three of the four corners at this junction. The others were the Spread Eagle and the Bulls Head. The latter closed in September 1958 and the building became part of Martin and Newby's shop.

The entrance to Cox Lane (left) at the junction of Tacket Street
and Orwell Place was much narrower when this photograph was
taken in the 1930s. Brown and Bradbrook were pawnbrokers who
also had premises in Friars Street, St Helens Street and Regent
Street. The buildings on the right are still standing.
(Guy Maynard, Colchester and Ipswich Museum Service)

Permit Office Street in the mid-1930s. The street was behind St Pancras Church and became part of the Cox Lane car park. When the area was cleared in the 1930s, most residents were moved to new council housing on the edge of town. The tower in the background was at the fire station in Bond Street. *(Guy Maynard, Colchester and Ipswich Museum Service)*

Children with an ice cream salesman at the corner of Little Barclay Street and Permit Office Street in the 1930s.
(Guy Maynard, Colchester and Ipswich Museum Service)

Tacket Street in the 1930s looking towards Cox Lane. All the buildings on the left have been demolished including the Tankard public house, which opened in 1736 and was rebuilt in 1802. The building on the extreme left was the Salvation Army Citadel. In 1994, the Salvation Army moved to Woodbridge Road. *(Guy Maynard, Colchester and Ipswich Museum Service)*

A similar view of Tacket Street to the one above in July 2011. *(DK)*

Tacket Street from the junction with Cox Lane (right) and Foundation Street (left) in the mid-1930s. When this photo was taken, the shops on the right were starting to be demolished.

When the shops in the photograph on the left were demolished there was a clear view of the Tacket Street Congregational Church, which opened in January 1858. The upper parts of the towers were removed in the 1970s. The pawnbroker's sign (top right) is featured in the photograph on page 76. This photograph was taken in the mid-1930s shortly after demolition was completed.

This photo was taken in March 1994 from over the Bishop's Hill area. Since then, the remains of the Ransomes, Sims and Jefferies site (left foreground) and the college buildings (centre right) have been demolished. Most of the buildings around the north quay of the dock have also been replaced. *(DK)*

ALPE ST

Bond Street fire station in the 1950s. This fire station was built in 1899. When the brigade moved in they were equipped with two steam pumps, a first aid machine, two manual pumps and three hose trucks. In November 1963, a new fire station opened up on Colchester Road but the Bond Street station remained in use until a new town centre station was opened on Princes Street on 15 July 1982.

Firefighters at the Bond Street fire station on a horse-drawn steam pump in the early years of the 20th century. The brigade did not have a motorised fire tender until February 1918.

Fore Street at the junction with Lower Orwell Street in 1890.

Fore Street in 1961. H and R Sneezum's shop on the right was at the junction of Lower Orwell Street. Sneezum's were photographic dealers, gunsmiths, sports outfitters and, until around World War II, pawnbrokers.

Fore Street in June 1961 as the street was being prepared for the visit of Queen Elizabeth who was due to formally open the Civic College. Fore Street was part of the route the Queen took to tour the town. Her visit included the Cornhill as well as Portman Road football ground where she was greeted by thousands of school children. The shops in this photo included Martin and Newby's ironmongers (left).

Fore Street in 1961. Star Lane now cuts across Fore Street where the trolley bus was. The establishments (from right to left) were: a women's outfitter, the Lucullas café and Smyth Brothers builder's merchants and ironmongers. This photograph was taken looking towards Eagle Street.

Fore Street from near Salthouse Street in an undated photograph probably taken in the 1880s. The Lion and Lamb public house at the junction of Fore Street and Angel Lane is in the centre.

The Angel Inn at the corner of Angel Lane and St Clements Church Lane was in poor condition when this photograph was taken in the 1890s. The building, also featured in the photograph above, is thought to have dated from the 15th century.
(Harry Walters)

A Victorian view of Fore Street taken from the junction of Salthouse Street. The Fore Street Baths is in the centre background. The baths and swimming pool were opened in 1894 providing an important facility for those who lived in the nearby poor housing, which was built without plumbing. Felix Thornley Cobbold, an Ipswich banker, a member of the brewing family and vice president of the Swimming Club, donated not only the site of the baths but also £1,200 towards construction. The council funded the rest of the work, which totalled £4,300. Felix Cobbold became Mayor in 1896–7 (see pages 168–71). The Angel Inn and the Lion and Lamb public houses are in the background.

The Fore Street swimming pool, with a viewing balcony above the changing cubicles, pictured shortly after the official opening in 1894. *(William Vick)*

Fore Street looking towards Salthouse Street in 1934. The Old Neptune Inn on the left was originally a merchant's house with parts dating from both the 15th and 16th century. In the 18th century it became an inn and remained either a beer house or inn until 1937. In 1947 it was derelict and restored as a private house. The entrance to Salthouse Street near the second post on the left was widened in the 1950s. *(Guy Maynard, Colchester and Ipswich Museum Service)*

A similar view of Fore Street in January 2011. *(DK)*

Fore Street in 1934. Church Street (renamed Grimwade Street) is to the left. A Salvation Army hostel was built on the left of this view. The building in the distant background, at the junction of Back Hamlet, was the Earl Grey public house, which closed in 1949.
(Guy Maynard, Colchester and Ipswich Museum Service)

Barnard Brothers shop at the junction of Church Street in the 1920s. The shop – which sold animal food stuff, hay and straw – was opened in October 1908 by Harry and Tom Barnard.

The Social Settlement was located on Fore Street, close to the Duke Street junction. It opened in the late 1890s as a community centre for the thousands of residents who lived in the area. After the death of the Social Settlement's founder, Congregationalist Daniel Ford Goddard, the settlement was closed. In the 1920s, the main hall of the community centre was converted into the Empire cinema and film shows were regularly held there. The Empire was known affectionately as the 'Tuppenny Rush'. The building was demolished in the 1950s. *(Harry Walters)*

Fore Street from near the Duke Street roundabout in October 1963. The entrance to the University Campus Suffolk is now where the cars are parked on the left. A block of flats called Neptune Square has replaced the large maltings building on the left. The vehicle on the right was being used by men removing trolley bus wires (see also page 35). *(Alan Valentine)*

A trolley bus at
the Duke Street
roundabout in
April 1963. The
roundabout was
removed from
this junction
between 2010
and 2011.
(Alan Valentine)

A similar view in March 2011. *(DK)*

These buildings stood on Fore Hamlet close to Duke Street. This photograph was taken in the mid-1930s. The maltings buildings on Fore Street, featured on page 88, are in the distant background. *(Guy Maynard, Colchester and Ipswich Museum Service)*

January 1963: one of the town's trolley buses passing the Gardener's Arms public house, at the junction of Fore Hamlet and Bishops Hill, after a fall of snow. *(Alan Valentine)*

Albion Street ran from the junction of Bishops Hill and Fore Hamlet to John Street (now part of Duke Street). The large gas holder at the gasworks was demolished in 1977.

(Guy Maynard, Colchester and Ipswich Museum Service)

Bishops Hill in March 1935. The White Elm public house stood halfway up the hill on the left. It closed in March 1965. Myrtle Road is to the right.

(Guy Maynard, Colchester and Ipswich Museum Service)

A group of wonderful characters gathering near East Court, off Regent Street, during the mid-1930s. This area was known as the Potteries. The area received its name because there were several potteries around Rope Walk at the time. The Potteries was part of the St Clements area, which was bound approximately by St Helens Street, Fore Street, Bishops Hill and the dock. Much of the area was overcrowded and the living conditions were poor. Most was demolished by the end of the 1930s and the residents were moved to new council housing estates on the edge of town.

(Guy Maynard, Colchester and Ipswich Museum Service)

Rope Walk in 1934. This picture was taken close to Eagle Street looking east. *(Guy Maynard, Colchester and Ipswich Museum Service)*

A view to the east along Woodhouse Street in the Potteries area in 1935. The Suffolk New College and its approach road are located here now.

(Guy Maynard, Colchester and Ipswich Museum Service)

The Suffolk New College in March 2011. *(DK)*

The Dock and Waterfront

The dock and New Cut in March 1994. When the Ipswich dock
was opened in 1842, it was the largest enclosed dock in the country.
To create the dock, New Cut (foreground) was excavated to take
the flow of the River Orwell. *(DK)*

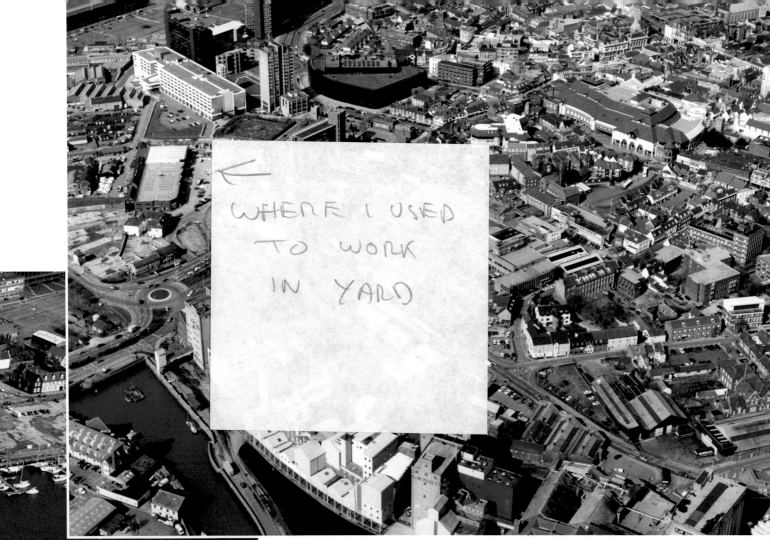

(handwritten annotations on photograph:) WHERE I USED TO WORK IN YARD

(handwritten annotations:) WHERE DAD WORKED

The close proximity between the dock and the town centre is illustrated in this aerial view taken over New Cut in March 1994. The granaries of the Cranfield Brothers and R and W Paul are in the foreground. Christchurch Mansion, with its acres of garden, was officially open the former Prime Minister Harold Wilson in 1977. See page 69. The Buttermarket Shopping Centre is top right.

The sailing ship, *Artemis*, at the Stoke Bridge end of the dock in 1897. This photograph was taken from Stoke Quay as horses and wagons line up along New Cut East. *(Harry Walters)*

➤

St Peter's Dock in the 1890s. The iron Stoke Bridge in the background opened on 19 June 1819 replacing a stone bridge, which had been washed away during a flood in April 1818. The iron bridge was eventually replaced in April 1925 by the present one (see page 130). The maltings building (left) was converted to barracks during the Napoleonic Wars. The central building was the Eastern Union Mills before it was replaced by yeast manufacturers British Fermentation Products Ltd. In 2002, the site became home to a skate park. *(Harry Walters)*

A busy scene close to Stoke Bridge in October 1967 as lorries were being loaded from the premises of R and W Paul (left). This photograph was taken after a high tide had flooded the quay. The area is now protected by a flood wall. *(Alan Valentine)*

Pleasure craft in New Cut in 1910. This view is taken
from the site of the original lock, which was opened in
1842. In July 1881, the present-day lock opened to
replace the old one and to provide ships with an easier
route into the dock. When this photograph was taken
there was a tree-lined promenade along New Cut East.
(Leonard Woolf, Ipswich Maritime Trust)

The paddle steamer *Orwell* setting off on a trip down the River Orwell circa 1895. On the right is the original opening to the lock. The buildings in the distant background were located on the dock near Stoke Bridge. *(Harry Walters)*

This photograph illustrates how the dock area was a mixture of trade and leisure in 1920. The view is taken looking towards the lock gates as timber was being unloaded at the South West Quay. The trees of the promenade are on the right.
(Leonard Woolf, Ipswich Maritime Trust)

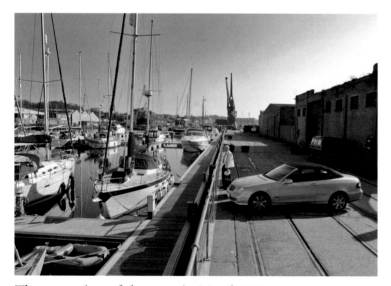

The same view of the quay in March 2011. *(DK)*

Workers with timber at the dock in the late 1920s. The wagon in the foreground belonged to contractors who were based at 27 Key Street.

The Ipswich Malting Company's premises on Stoke Quay in 1900. These huge buildings, similar to the Felaw Street Maltings, were demolished in the 1970s.

A view of the island site in the 1970s as the Ipswich Malting Company's building (foreground) was being demolished. The Felaw Street Maltings building is centre right. *(Fred Bridges)*

A panoramic view from the top of Cranfield's silo, close to Stoke Bridge, in the late 1960s. The barges in the dock were used to store grain. They were moored alongside what was known as Flint Wharf. William Brown's timber yard occupied a huge part of the island. New Cut East runs through the centre of the picture with the huge gas holder at the gasworks in the background. The massive Ipswich Malting Company building on the right was demolished in the 1970s. The Felaw Street Maltings, in the right background, stood empty for many years, before being converted into offices. *(Bob Graham)*

The sailing ship, *Gratitude*, at the dock in the original lock channel in the 1890s. The buildings in the background to the right were part of the Ransomes, Sims and Jefferies site between Duke Street and the quay.

In this view from Stoke Quay in 1960, most of the building featured belonged to the Cranfield Brothers, flour millers.

(Stuart Grimwade, Ipswich Maritime Trust)

A similar view from Stoke Quay taken on 19 January 2011. *(DK)*

A locomotive pulling wagons along New Cut East in January 1964. *(Alan Valentine)*

The new lock was opened on 27 July 1881. A ceremony equipped with a grandstand was held at the site and the Mayor, local Members of Parliament, the general manager of the Great Eastern Railway Company and the president of the Board of Trade made their entrance on the *Glen Rosa*, a London Steamship Company paddle steamer. The *Glen Rosa* sailed through the lock as cannons fired and crowds of onlookers watched. This photograph from the East bank suggests that the *Glen Rosa* turned in the dock and stopped in the lock for further ceremony. It was a great day for Ipswich as on the same day the Post Office on the Cornhill and the Museum in High Street were also opened.

The last sailing ship to deliver grain to the dock was the clipper *Abraham Ryberg* in 1939. The ship had sailed from Spencer Gulf, Australia on 18 February and berthed at Cliff Quay on 18 June. After unloading part of her cargo, the ship moved into the dock on 30 June. This photograph was taken on 16 July 1939 as *Stronghold*, the Ipswich Dock Commission tug, towed the ship back out through the lock. The work of tug master James Orvis was watched by a large crowd as the huge ship made its way from Ipswich for the last time.
(Ipswich Maritime Trust)

The lock in 1910. The barges on the left belonged to E Packard and Company
who produced fertiliser at their works in Coprolite Street (see page 109).

Barges in the lock in 1920.

A panoramic view of the port from the top of a gas holder at the gasworks in 1953 (see page 110). The engineering works of Ransomes & Rapier and Cocksedge and Company Ltd are in the top right corner. The Stoke Bathing Place (see page 137) extended into the river close to the Ransomes & Rapier works. Cliff Quay is top left and the lock into the dock is in the right foreground.
(Frank Symonds)

The River Orwell from the lock in 1910. Cliff Quay now stands
on the land in the left background. Work started in 1923
and the first quay opened in 1925.

In 1900, thousands of spectators filled the bank near the lock gate's end of New Cut to watch an annual regatta. The shelter featured was known as the Umbrella. It remained until the 1950s. The Cobbold brewery at Cliff Quay is in the background to the right.

Draymen with their wagons and Suffolk Punch horses at Cobbold's Brewery, Cliff Quay in February 1935. The horses were stabled at the brewery and kept in a field at the junction of Cliff Lane and Landseer Road. Brewing took place at this site from 1746 using water from Holywells. The brewery in the background was built between 1894 and 1896 on the site of the old one and it was extended in later years. Cobbold's Brewery merged with the Tollemache Brewery in the 1950s.

Parts of the gasworks and Ransomes, Sims and Jefferies engineering works from a gas holder in 1953. The gasworks moved to this site in 1822 from a small site between Carr Street and Old Foundry Road. The location by the river meant coal could be conveniently shipped to the site. Ransomes' original Ipswich works was on Old Foundry Road (St Margaret's Ditches) but they began the move to the new site in 1841 and their original site closed in 1849. *(Frank Symonds)*

A view across the dock in the 1890s taken from Eagle Wharf looking towards the town. *(Harry Walters)*

The dock from a gas holder. This undated photograph probably dates back to the 1920s. The buildings in the right foreground were parts of the gasworks and Ransomes, Sims and Jefferies (see page 109).

The gas holder at the gasworks from near Harland Street around 1959. *(Ipswich Maritime Trust)*

A view across the dock in 2005 from flats built on the former gasworks site close to Patterson Road. The tower and spire of St Mary-le-Tower Church is in the centre background. *(DK)*

In 2005 the skyline along the north side of dock was about to change. Most of the buildings that once belonged to the companies R and W Paul and Cranfield were replaced by residential and leisure buildings. *(DK)*

Edward Packard's fertiliser works is on the left of this view taken from across the dock circa 1908. Coprolite Street (left) dates back to 1850 when the works were set up. Edward Packard was an agricultural chemist from Saxmundham who used the area to dissolve ground coprolites in sulphuric acid to make artificial fertiliser.

The company also owned an establishment in Bramford where they were able to use the River Orwell and the River Gipping to transport company barges. The tower of Holy Trinity Church in Fore Hamlet is behind Packard's works. The university building is now on the extreme left of this view. *(Charles Trudgill)*

Neptune Quay in the early 1960s from near the junction with Coprolite Street. The silo in the background belonged to Eastern Counties Farmers Ltd. The university was built on this site. The iron building built over the quay is shown in the Edwardian photograph above. *(Fred Bridges)*

Neptune Quay in 2009. The university building in the centre opened in September 2008.
Coprolite Street is between the university and the building on the right. *(DK)*

The dock circa 1970 as the barge *Ena*, which belonged to R and W Paul,
sails towards the Stoke Bridge end of the dock. *Ena* was built at Harwich in 1906.

Neptune Quay from the island, 9 May 1964. The buildings (left to right) were then occupied by William Brown and Company (Ipswich) Ltd builders' merchants, Isaac Lord coal merchants, the British Oil and Cake Mills Ltd seed crushers store and J Whitmore Ltd ships' chandlers. The tower of St Clements church is just visible in the right background.
(Alan Valentine)

Barge hands by the quay in 1930. Buildings in the background are featured in the photograph above from 1964.
(Titshall Brothers)

The quay at Ipswich Dock in September 1964 from near the Custom House. The silo in the background belonged to Eastern Counties Farmers, a farming co-operative which established a compound feed mill on the site in 1954. The university building now stands on this site.
(Alan Valentine)

Men performing the back-breaking job of unloading sacks of grain at Albion Wharf circa 1930. The area was later renamed Regatta Quay. *(Titshall Brothers)*

A wall at this grain silo at Albion Wharf collapsed in 1897 spilling hundreds of tons of grain into the dock and blocking the quay. *(Harry Walters)*

The following is an extract from the March 1897 *London Corn Circular*:

'Messrs Cranfield Bros have adjoining their steam flour mill a large warehouse, with an elevation of some 80 feet and walls two feet thick, but there were no floors or piers to equalise the weight. Girders ran from side to side, but not from back to front. The structure was packed full of wheat. A perpendicular crack from top to bottom was noticed some time before the collapse and this was sufficiently ominous to put a stop to all traffic on the quay. A nut was then seen to fall from one of the fly-rods in the wall, which cracked in all directions; the top appeared to fall inwards, the middle bulged out and all came down with a terrific crash upon the quay.'

In September 2009, Regatta Quay is clearly a residential area as well as a centre for leisure and recreation. *(DK)*

The island site at the Stoke Bridge end in 1970 from a silo in the dock. A grain ship was being unloaded. New Cut is top right.
(Ruth Sergeant, Ipswich Maritime Trust)

Loading a lorry at Cranfields Mill around 1970. *(Ruth Sergeant, Ipswich Maritime Trust)*

Cranfields Mill circa 1960. *(Brian Jepson, Ipswich Maritime Trust)*

Barges near Cranfields Mill in the 1890s. *(John Wiggin)*

St Peter's Wharf and Stoke Bridge Wharf from Stoke Bridge in the 1890s. *(Harry Walters)*

Barges about to pass under Stoke Bridge in the 1890s. On 14 September 1793, trade opened on the river and there were fifteen locks on the River Gipping to Stowmarket. The building of the dock and the railway saw trade drop in the second half of the 19th century and by 1900 there was little or no trade on the Gipping. Navigation ended in 1922. The building on the left used to be a malting and was later used as barracks during the Napoleonic Wars. It has been converted to flats. *(Harry Walters)*

An aerial view from over Vernon Street in March 1994. Stoke Bridge is in the bottom left corner. The building featured in the photograph on the facing page is the red-tiled structure next to the bridge. St Peter's Church is in the centre and the Buttermarket Shopping Centre is at the top on the right. *(DK)*

This panorama is from two negatives taken from the top of the R and W Paul silo near Stoke Bridge in the mid-1960s. Commercial Road, renamed Grafton Way, runs from the bottom left corner towards Princes Street. The Greyfriars development is top right and Greyfriars Road bottom right. Cardinal Park was built in the centre of this view. The 'Lower Yard' of the railway (see photographs on pages 132–3) and the River Orwell are on the left. *(Mike Farthing)*

Buildings on Commercial Road were badly damaged by fire on 18 March 1968. The fire started at Wellard Tyres, a site which is now part of the Cardinal Park complex. The building on the left of the photograph on page 122 once housed the town's horse-drawn trams. The rails were still visible when the area was cleared to build the Cardinal Park complex.

(Alan Valentine)

Stoke Bridge from the River Orwell circa 1890. *(John Wiggin)*

A view of the premises of British Fermentation Products Ltd from the bank of the River Orwell near Burrell Road in 1960. The mills and silos of Cranfields and R and W Paul are in the background. The tower of St Peter's Church is on the left. *(Brian Jepson, Ipswich Maritime Trust)*

Key Street from the junction with Lower Orwell Street in the mid-1930s. R and W Paul built a silo on the site in the right foreground in 1962. The Custom House is in the background.

(Guy Maynard, Colchester and Ipswich Museum Service)

A German bomb that was dropped in an air raid during World War II damaged buildings in Key Street on 27 February 1941. The damage to this silo caused grain to spill onto the street, blocking the road by the St Mary-at-the-Quay Church, the wall of which is on the right. Most of the windows were blown out of the church and there was structural damage. A report written at the time said:

'A Heinkel III (bomber) at low altitude flying west to east dropped four 250 kg bombs and machine gunned the streets. Bombs fell on Key Street – one on Paul's, another on Kerridge Brothers bakers, a third on Paul's and fourth on 74 Fore Street. A boy was killed.'

Foundation Street from near the junction of Lower Brook Street. The road behind the camera to College Street was then called Bank Street (see sign top right). The tall building in the distant background at the junction of Orwell Place was the Unicorn Brewery. It closed as a brewery in 1923. The building has since been converted to flats.

Foundation Street (right), Lower Brook Street (left) and Star Lane from the tower of St Mary-at-the-Quay Church on 1 March 2006. The former brewery building featured in the picture at the top of the page is top right. The Buttermarket Shopping Centre roof is top left. *(DK)*

The Half Moon public house at the junction of Lower Brook Street (left) and Foundation Street circa 1912. The Half Moon was built in the 15th century and had a fine carved corner post. It was demolished in 1960. The buildings on the right in this picture are featured on the left of the photograph at the top of page 126.

The Half Moon Inn at the junction of Lower Brook Street and Foundation Street was being demolished for redevelopment in March 1960.

St Mary-at-the-Quay Church in the 1950s from a silo at the dock. At that time, Star Lane was very narrow and linked to Lower Orwell Street. The building in front of the church (bottom left) was the Sea Horse public house, which closed in the mid-1970s. The tower of St Clements Church is top right.

These buildings at the junction of Lower Brook Street (right) and Foundation Street were demolished in the 1960s. Star Lane now passes on the left of this view. This photograph was taken around 1960. One of the grain silos at the dock is in the left background.
(Richard Pipe)

Foundation Street at the junction of Star Lane (left) and Turret Lane in the 1950s. St Mary-at-the-Quay Church with its 73-foot tower was then topped by a wooden cupola containing a Sanctus bell. Other than the church, all the buildings between the camera and College Street have been demolished. Star Lane is now a busy one-way road that runs from St Peter's Church and carries traffic through to Waterworks Street and Grimwade Street. Cranfields Mill in College Street is in the background. This building was retained in the redevelopment of the dock area. The Sea Horse public house (featured on page 128) is on the far right. The silo in the left background was demolished in 2006.

A similar view including St Mary-at-the-Quay Church in April 2011. *(DK)*

Over Stoke

Stoke Bridge in September 1963. The R and W Paul building behind the bus was destroyed by fire in April 2000. The tower of St Peter's Church is on the left. *(Alan Valentine)*

In December 1982, work began to dual the Stoke Bridge river crossing. A double roundabout system was also built on the town side of the bridge as part of a traffic management scheme.

Vernon Street looking towards Stoke Bridge in October 1964. The shop on the right was Alfred Potter's drapers shop. Further along the street was Laurence Wilden's greengrocers and Ernest Gilbert's butchers shop. *(Alan Valentine)*

A similar view of Vernon Street in February 2011. *(DK)*

The photographs on these two pages are taken from different vantage points on Stoke Hill in the 1890s; together they form a panorama. The terrace of houses (left) is still on Burrell Road. The house in the foreground is located on Willoughby Road.

The tower of St Nicholas Church is in the centre and the spire of St Mary-le-Tower Church is in the background. The large building at the rail yard was a shed for goods. The same building features in the 1960s photograph on pages 122–3.

The rail yard between the River Orwell and Commercial Road was full of wagons. The smoke is from chimneys in Burrell Road.

The tower of St Peter's Church and Stoke Bridge are featured in this view looking towards the dock.
(Harry Walters)

The works of engineering companies Ransomes & Rapier and Cocksedge and Company dominate this aerial view. The photograph was probably taken in 1976. The gas holder at the town's gasworks (right foreground) was demolished in 1977. The construction work has just started on Stoke High School (top centre) in Maidenhall Approach. This site was opened in the late 1970s. The West Bank Terminal is centre left and expansion work was then under way.

The history of Ransomes & Rapier in Ipswich began in July 1869. Generations of local people were employed by the company, which worked on worldwide projects. In 1987, 'R&R' was closed by Robert Maxwell's Hollis Group, the parent company at the time. Cocksedge and Company began in Suffolk in 1879 and closed in December 1985.

In the bottom left corner is the Tolly Cobbold brewery at Cliff Quay.

A photograph taken at the same time as the picture on the facing page. Wherstead Road is across the top right corner. Cliff Quay top left and the lock is centre left.

Bell Lane in the mid-1930s. The Boar's Head Inn, which closed in 1939, in Boar's Head Lane (now part of Austin Street) is in the background. Little Whip Street is to the left. All these buildings have gone.
(Guy Maynard, Colchester and Ipswich Museum Service)

Wherstead Road on 31 July 1965. The public house in the background was the Eagle Tavern at the corner of Bath Street. The tavern closed in 1977.
(Alan Valentine)

Stoke Bathing Place with Cliff Quay in the background circa 1925. The bathing place was built around 1850. It was a walled-off area of the River Orwell (see page 107) and the water was changed every day by controlling the tide with sluice gates. The diving platform featured in this photo was added in 1906 and taken down in 1927. This bathing area was in use until it was badly damaged during the East Coast flood of 1953. This and the problem of purifying water during the polio epidemic saw the end of the facility. The site is now part of the West Bank Terminal.

Members of the Ipswich Borough Police Force during a training session at Stoke Bathing Place in 1908. The Ipswich Swimming Club house was built in 1886.

St Mary Stoke School, on Belstead Road, stood opposite Rectory Road in front of St Mary Stoke Church. The building on the right of those in the foreground was once the Stoke Parish Poor House. When the Ipswich Union Workhouse was built in Great Whip Street it became part of St Mary Stoke School. The buildings were demolished shortly after this photograph was taken in November 1964. Until then they had been used by scouts and guides. The church hall and car park were built on this site. The building in the right background replaced those in the photograph below.

(Alan Valentine)

Stoke Street at the junction with Belstead Road in 1938. Boar's Head Lane (now Austin Street) was off to the right. St Mary Stoke Church is off the photograph to the left.

(Guy Maynard, Colchester and Ipswich Museum Service)

Cliff Quay power station from Bourne Bridge in the 1960s. Work first started on the site in 1939 but was stopped at the outbreak of World War II. Work restarted in 1945 and the site was opened in 1949 at a cost of approximately £8 million. In September 1982, power generation ceased after a fire. In the end, the massive building was demolished first and its landmark chimneys were brought down with explosives in November 1994.
(Harry Dedman)

The turbine hall at Cliff Quay power station.

On 20 September 1970, a huge fire broke out at the Ipswich Malting Company premises on New Cut West. This photograph was taken from Bulstrode Road as the fire threatened houses. See also pictures of the maltings on page 101. *(Alan Valentine)*

The fire at the maltings from near the junction of Austin Street and Vernon Street. *(Alan Valentine)*

There was a horse-drawn bus service from the Cornhill to the Ostrich public house near Bourne Bridge when this photograph was taken in 1898. *(Harry Walters)*

The Ostrich public house on Bourne Hill in September 1963. This Grade II listed building dates back to the 16th century. It was renamed the Oyster Reach in 1995. *(Alan Valentine)*

The Ostrich as seen from Bourne Hill in the 1890s with the River Orwell in the background. *(Harry Walters)*

Around the Town

In 1795, barracks were built on a site just north of the junction between St Matthews Street, London Road and Norwich Road. The junction is still known as Barrack Corner. Brick buildings stood on three sides of the site until around 1930 when they were mostly demolished and Geneva Road and Cecil Road were built. At first, cavalry troops were based in the town but, in the second part of the 19th century, the Royal Field Artillery and the Royal Horse Artillery were based there. This photograph of troops at the barracks was taken in the 1890s. *(Harry Walters)*

An aerial view of the barracks area probably from around 1920. Orford Street is across the left corner. Berners Street is in the top right corner and the Anglesea Road Hospital (see page 145) is located at the top.

An aerial view of the former barracks area in September 1963. Geneva Road and Cecil Road are located centre left. Berners Street runs from the bottom left corner. The Anglesea Road Hospital and Ipswich School, with its cricket pitch, are top right. The Ipswich Museum buildings are partly hidden in the foreground by the wing tip of the aircraft.

Building work on the former barracks site in the 1930s. Some of the barracks' buildings were still in the process of being demolished when this photograph was taken.

The view is towards St Matthews Street. The chimney in the background was at St Matthews Baths and Berners Street is on the left. *(Guy Maynard, Colchester and Ipswich Museum Service)*

The officers' mess at the barracks soon before demolition. This building is close to the centre of the photograph at the top of page 143. *(Guy Maynard, Colchester and Ipswich Museum Service)*

The entrance to Anglesea Road Hospital from Berners Street in the 1960s. Anglesea Road Hospital opened in 1836. It cost around £2,500 which was provided by public subscription. The original two-storey building featured with its four columns had a floor added in 1869. By 1988 all services were moved to Heath Road Hospital. Most of the buildings were demolished and the original building was converted into a nursing home that opened in August 1991.

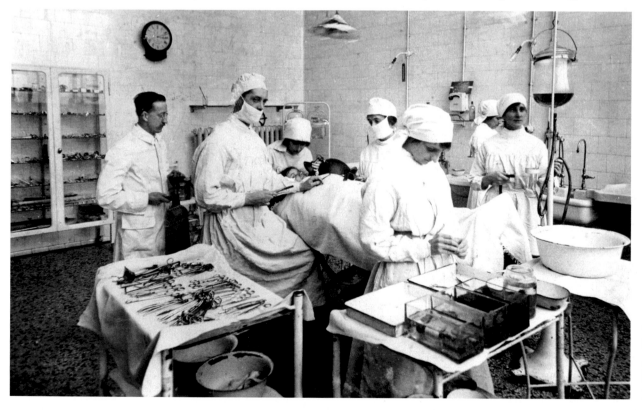

An operating theatre at the Anglesea Road Hospital in the 1920s.

A Tithe Gift Sale at the Cattle Market in April 1933. The sale was organised by Bond and Son and Spurling and Hempson. The houses in the background (to the left) were located on Friarsbridge Road at the junction with Portman Road.

This pair of photographs of the Cattle Market was taken in the 1890s. The market moved to this site in 1856 from a town centre site known since as the Old Cattle Market. Princes Street is in the foreground. The buildings in the left background were on Portman Road and in the distance is St Matthews Church tower and the spire of the church at Barrack Corner. The Cattle Market closed on this site in 1985.
(Harry Walters)

An aerial view taken in March 1965 with the Cattle Market site, Portman Road and the Ipswich Town Football Club ground in the left foreground. At that time, Civic Drive was being cut through from St Matthews Street to Princes Street. Cumberland Towers at the junction of Norwich Road and Bramford Road (top centre) was nearing completion. The two insurance company office blocks on Civic Drive were both completed by 1971.

This fancy dress contestant was taking part in an event at the Portman Road sports ground circa 1900. The line of spectators is located where the north stand of the football stadium is today. The houses on the left are on Alderman Road.

The chimney at the Constantine Road power station stood almost 179 feet above the town, four feet taller than the spire of St Mary-le-Tower Church. It was twelve feet square inside at the top and at that point the walls were a foot thick. The site included a 'refuse destructor' to deal with the town's rubbish but, at the time of this photo (1958), work to demolish the structure had just started.

This is the view from the top of the new chimney of the Constantine Road power station circa 1903. In the foreground is the area now known as the grounds of Ipswich Town Football Club, then known as the East Suffolk Cricket and Football Ground. This recreation area was opened on 2 June 1888 as part of a host of celebrations to mark Queen Victoria's birthday. The power station, workshop, car shed and offices were built by Kenney's of Ipswich for around £34,000 with work starting on 20 October 1902. The power station for the new tram service meant that industry, offices and homes would be connected for the first time. Portman Road runs across the picture. Portmans Walk (renamed Sir Alf Ramsey Way) and Alderman Road are on the left.

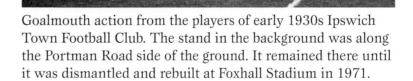

Goalmouth action from the players of early 1930s Ipswich Town Football Club. The stand in the background was along the Portman Road side of the ground. It remained there until it was dismantled and rebuilt at Foxhall Stadium in 1971.

Match day at Ipswich Town Football Club in August 2007. *(DK)*

Services were held all over the country on the day of the funeral of King Edward VII on 20 May 1910. The Territorial Army and the boy scouts held an open-air memorial service on what is now the main pitch at Ipswich Town Football Club.

The Suffolk Stallion Show at the Ipswich Town Football Club ground in March 1956. This area is the practice pitch at the club. The building in the background was Russell House. Endeavor House, the home of the Suffolk County Council's offices, now stands on that site.

An inspection of members of the Ipswich Borough Police Force on the practice pitch at Ipswich Town Football Club in the 1950s. In the background is the former power station.

The annual junior school sports were held on the main pitch at Ipswich Town Football Club. This was the start of a race in June 1966. The Churchman's stand is in the background.

This photo from the 1920s illustrates the premises of Reavell and Company in Ranelagh Road. The engineering company was formed in 1898 by William Reavell, who later received a knighthood, on a site purchased from the Great Eastern Railway Company. His engineering works were finally demolished in 2006 and the site has since been redeveloped mainly with flats.

A similar view of Ranelagh Road in February 2011. *(DK)*

Elephants from Chipperfield's Circus parading past Reavell's site in Ranelagh Road on 27 May 1955. The circus had arrived at Ipswich Station and was making its way to a site, regularly used by visiting circuses, at the junction with London Road.

The foundry at Reavell's works on Ranelagh Road circa 1920.

Norwich Road looking out of town, near the rail bridge in 1904. A tram car from the new electric tram service and its crew are under the bridge. The electric power lines under the bridge were offset to keep passengers on the top deck away from the live wires.

Members of the fire brigade with their horse-drawn steam pumps preparing to move off at the Norwich Road rail bridge in the annual Lifeboat Saturday parade circa 1910. The event was a procession through town to raise money for the lifeboat service. The fire brigade was joined on the parade by soldiers from the town's barracks. The lettering on the bridge warns tram passengers: 'To keep their seats while passing under the bridge'.

It was a busy day for the bookies at the Ipswich Racecourse when this Victorian photograph was taken. Racing had been held at this site since 1710. The track was 2½ miles long and it was generally officers from the cavalry at the Ipswich barracks and the local gentry who took part. The 'lower classes' watched from around the track on a site that is now approximately bound by Felixstowe Road, Lindbergh Road, Nacton Road and Levington Road. The last steeplechase was in 1895 but flat racing continued until 29 March 1911. This area of Ipswich is still known as Racecourse but since 1921 it has been a housing development.

Nacton Road in the early 1930s. The Racecourse public house at the corner of Benacre Road closed in 2008. The building was demolished in 2009 and replaced by a supermarket.

The Broom Hill Pools complex opened in April 1938 and cost
£17,000 to build. During World War II the heating system was
removed. On hot summer days the pools were full to capacity with
visitors and huge queues formed along Sherrington Road. This
photograph was taken in the 1970s.

A very busy day at
Broom Hill Pools in the
summer of 1964.

A young swimmer
leaps from one of the
diving boards at
Broom Hill Pools in
August 1965.

Sandy Hill Lane, near Greenwich Farm, in the 1890s. This farmland on the fringe of Ipswich has now changed completely. Landseer Road now closely follows this route. The River Orwell is in the distant background and Cliff Quay is to the left of this view. *(Harry Walters)*

Landseer Road in February 2011 from near the same location as the photograph above. *(DK)*

The sugar beet factory off Sproughton Road from the air in September 1963. The factory was built in the mid-1920s and closed in 2001. The River Gipping is in the bottom right corner. Sproughton Road runs from left centre towards Bramford Road. The Boss Hall industrial site and a supermarket were built on the site beyond the railway line which runs across the centre of the picture.

The sugar beet harvest began in September and lasted through the winter. During harvest the roads around the sugar beet factory were busy with lorries loaded with the crop. This photograph was taken at the factory in the 1950s.

Bramford Road circa 1904. The electric trams came into service on this route in December 1903 and ran until 1926, when they were replaced with trolley buses. This tram and crew were near Kingston Road. The Bramford Road Methodist Church is in the background. *(Harry Walters)*

A similar view of Bramford Road in February 2011 with the Red Lion public house at the corner of Kingston Road on the left. *(DK)*

An accident in Bramford Road in the 1950s. This photograph was taken looking towards Norwich Road. The public house behind the overturned car was the Three Cups public house at the corner of Wellington Street, which closed in March 1962. The large buildings in the right background belonged to Alfred Gibbon's mill in Benezet Street.

The junction of Bramford Road and Wellington Street in February 2011. *(DK)*

This weir was where the Yarmouth Road sluice gates are now. This photograph from the 1890s captures the flow of the River Gipping into the River Orwell. In the picture, the Gipping flows off to the right behind the man standing on the bank. The Yarmouth Road bridge now crosses the water at that point.

The Gipping then flows under London Road to the weir at West End Road where the first of the locks was built to allow barges to travel along the river. The tannery, which was off Bramford Road, is in the background. The man in the picture is photographer Harry Walters who took several of the photographs in this book.

The Seven Arches Bridge crossed the River Orwell at London Road. This photograph from around 1908 was taken from near Ranelagh Road. The bridge was demolished in May 1959 and replaced with the present one, which now carries thousands of vehicles daily between the Hadleigh Road and Yarmouth Road junctions. *(Charles Trudgill)*

The Alderman Canal is off the river from near the end of Cullingham Road to Alderman Road (background). The chimney was at the Alderman Road laundry. This photograph was taken in the 1890s. *(Harry Walters)*

The River Gipping from the tow path near Riverside Road (left) around 1900. The river curves to the right beyond the trees and the tannery building, which stood between Riverside Road and Beaconsfield Road in the background. The sails of a windmill which stood in Tower Mill Road are in the centre. The mill tower, the last in Ipswich, was demolished in the 1950s. *(Harry Walters)*

The Withipoll Arms public house at the junction of Bolton Lane and Withipoll Street in the 1890s. It closed as a public house in September 1937 and has since been converted into a shop. *(Harry Walters)*

Felixstowe Road, at the cross roads with Hatfield Road (left) and Derby Road, in the late 1920s. The open-topped double-deck bus was heading for Felixstowe. *(Frederick Gillson)*

Pond Hall Farm stands close to the River Orwell at the end of Gainsborough Lane on the east side of the river. When this photograph was taken the farm was remote from the town. The Gainsborough housing estate was built nearby in the 1930s. In the early 1980s, the Orwell Bridge and A14 were constructed nearby. *(Harry Walters)*

The Orwell Bridge and river from Pond Hall Farm in 2007.
Work started on the bridge in 1979 and it was opened to traffic on 17 December 1982. *(DK)*

Christchurch Park

Members of the Ipswich Ramblers Cycling Club in front of Christchurch Mansion in 1897. Christchurch was originally the site of a 12th century Augustinian priory, which was disbanded by Henry VIII in his Dissolution of the Monasteries. The estate was seized for the crown but in 1545, the Withipoll family purchased it and, three years later, the mansion was built where the priory stood.

In 1735, the house was purchased by London merchant Claude Fonnereau. The last Fonnereau to live in the house was William Neale Fonnereau who offered the estate to the Ipswich Corporation for £50,000 but ratepayers voted against the purchase.

On 23 February 1895, wealthy businessman Felix Cobbold bought the mansion from the Fonnereau family who had already sold some land and planned to sell more for development. Felix Cobbold gave the mansion to the town on the condition that the Ipswich Corporation purchased the rest of the property and that the mansion was preserved. The central part of the park was purchased in the deal and the park was officially opened to the public on 11 April 1895.

This undated Victorian photograph of Christchurch Mansion was taken when the park was still privately owned. The Wolsey Gallery was built onto the rear of the mansion in 1931.

Sheep grazing near the mansion circa 1898. *(Harry Walters)*

Queen Victoria's Diamond Jubilee was celebrated in 1897. On 24 June, Mayor Felix Cobbold held a huge party on the park for children of elementary schools in the borough to celebrate the event. A reception was held by the mayor in front of the mansion. In the park there were steam roundabouts, swings and booths. The band of the Suffolk Regiment and the Stoke Excelsior Band provided music. Athletics races were held through the afternoon. A bugle sounded and 'scholars assembled for tea'. After singing the National Anthem, there was a march past with the mayor on the stand.

Children walking through the park during the Diamond Jubilee celebrations of June 1897. The round pond is in the background. *(Harry Walters)*

Some of the thousands of children who took part in the Diamond Jubilee celebrations in their best summer clothes. *(Harry Walters)*

A Memorial to Protestant martyrs was erected close to the Bolton Lane gate on the park in 1903. It was in memory of the nine Ipswich martyrs burnt at the stake under the reign of Mary I. The executions were mainly carried out on the Cornhill. This photograph of the memorial was taken in 2005. *(DK)*

St John's pupils
passing the round
pond during the
Diamond Jubilee
celebrations of 1897.
(Harry Walters)

Children pose for the camera during the Diamond Jubilee celebrations in 1897. The children on the right are featured in the photograph on page 168. *(Harry Walters)*

The lodge to the arboretum opposite Ipswich School on Henley Road. James Mann, photographed with his wife at their home in 1910, was head gardener of the Upper and Lower Arboretum. He later became the superintendent for all Ipswich parks. *(Charles Trudgill)*